Bipolar

Disorder

&

Me

Written & Illustrated by: *Lady Taylor*

Series 1

A.D.H.D. and Me
Attention Deficit Hyperactivity Disorder
ISBN: 978-0-6488270-5-4 (paperback)

Anxiety and Me
ISBN: 978-0-6488270-0-9 (paperback)

Bipolar Disorder and Me
ISBN: 978-0-6488270-6-1 (paperback)

Depression and Me
ISBN: 978-0-6488270-1-6 (paperback)

D.I.D. and Me
Dissociative Identity Disorder
ISBN: 978-0-6488270-4-7 (paperback)

OCD and Me
Obsessive Compulsive Disorder
 ISBN: 978-0-6488270-3-0 (paperback)

PTSD and Me
Post-Traumatic Stress Disorder
ISBN: 978-0-6488270-2-3 (paperback)

Appreciation & Gratitude

The most heartfelt thanks to my best friend/ hubby/ mad-scientist/ one-of-a-kind Gentleman - Lord Taylor. You have been consistantly there for me through all sad and glad, crazy and fazy, and just plain 'what the hay...?' times. Without you, I would not be able to share my gifts with anyone! You are so precious to me, and always will be...

To my good friend and consultant, Miss Jess... for all the years of 'trying' to keep me grounded, and all the hours we spent on the phone when I came down too fast... I love you for all your worth!

My Nanny June, for inspiring me to write and draw throughout my life... you and Grandad Del have been one of my most consistant souls and influences in both my creative and spiritual growth. Thank you for believing in me.

And to all of the mental health professionals whom helped me, and others, through our journey, and continue to do so. I am forever grateful for your strength. I hope my books serve as a light resource to aid people in understanding these conditions, and the support you provide for so many. THANK YOU!

Bipolar Disorder & Me

Trigger Warning

The contents of this book may be emotionally triggering to readers, due to sensitive subject matter and descriptive drawings.

Discretion Advised

Information gathered and presented as 'symptoms' within this book are true in nature to the peoples from whom the fictional characters are representative of. Symptoms may vary in nature dependant on individuals. Personal experiences may vary from those within these stories. By no means are they to be used as 'diagnostic criteria' or in replacement for professional medical assessments.

This means that we experience episodes of EXTREME excitement and hyperactivity or...

...episodes of depressive moods that can become so severe, that our actions become self-destructive or non-existent.

Our 'Episodes' refer to moments of consistent emotions. They can last anywhere between a couple of hours to several weeks. Depending on the severity of our condition.

The length of our 'episodes' lack consistency.

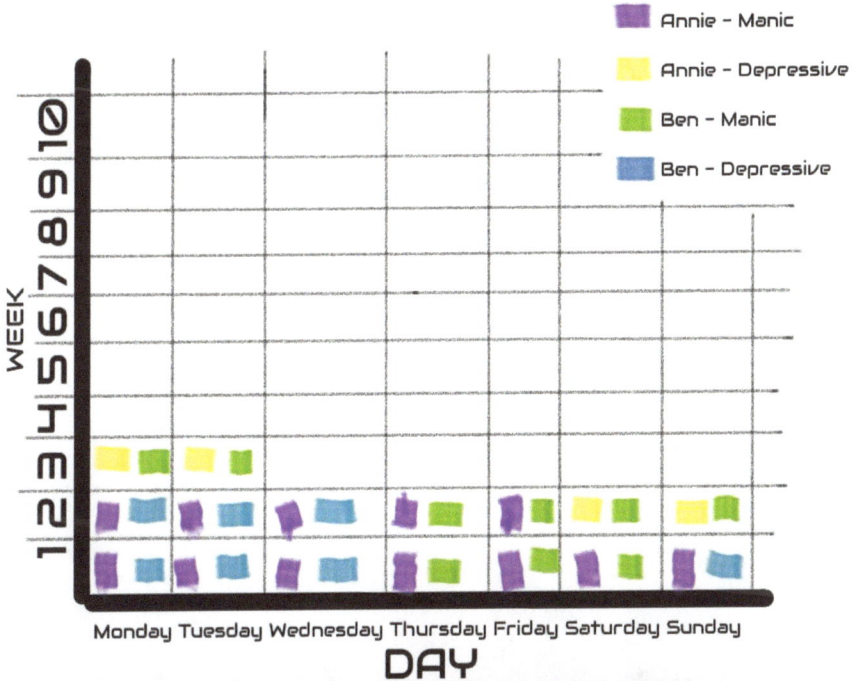

Legend:
- Annie – Manic
- Annie – Depressive
- Ben – Manic
- Ben – Depressive

Y-axis: WEEK (1 2 3 4 5 6 7 8 9 10)

X-axis: DAY — Monday Tuesday Wednesday Thursday Friday Saturday Sunday

At times we can be 'triggered' into a Manic or Depressive mood, depending on certain personal experiences, situations or our environment. Most of the time we switch from one extreme to another without notice; making it difficult to prepare or predict our episodes.

When we have a Manic episode
we can become hyperactive,
may make decisions without thinking
them through and act instinctively.

Our friends and family may know when we are in a Manic state. We might talk super fast.
Our mind will be working overtime and we tend to over-react emotionally.

I feel paranoid when I experience
a Manic episode.
This causes me to have moments of delusion,
restlessness and disorganised behaviour.
I find I tend to 'hear' and 'remember'
conversations and situations that didn't
actually happen as a result of stress.

Calming me down from a Manic episode is apparently very difficult because I get so immersed in the moment.

Medication is the main resource that controls my mood swings and helps me to think more clearly.

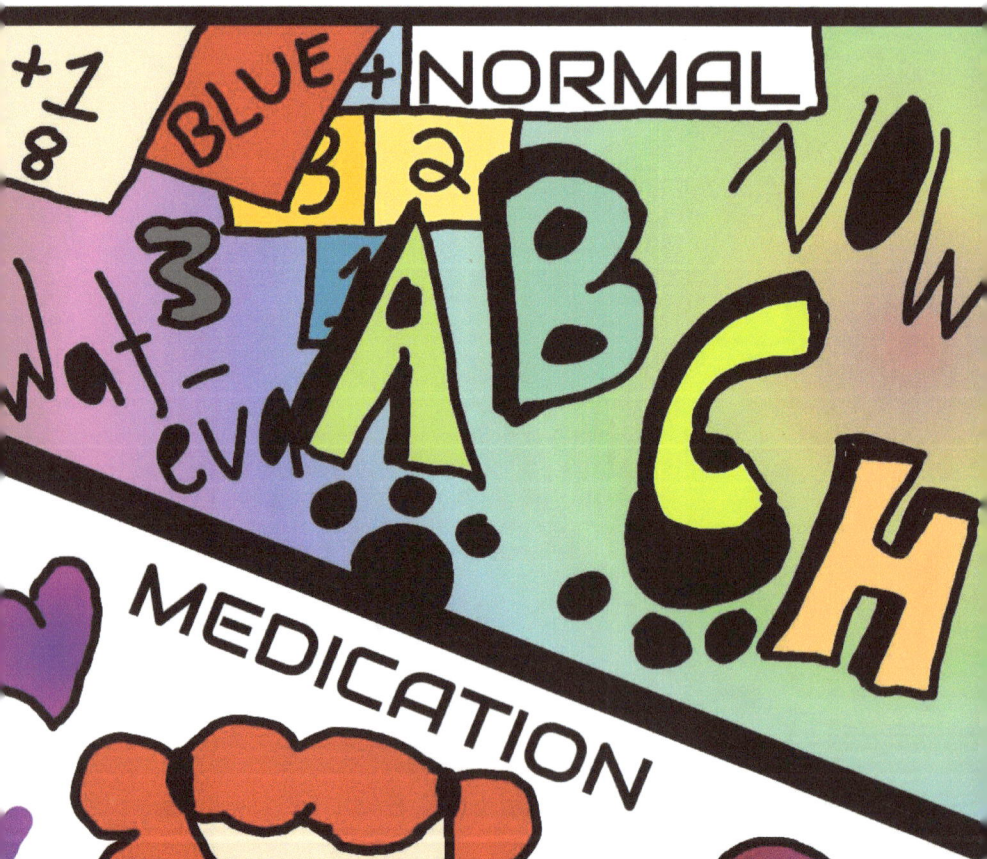

When Ben is in a manic state, he tends to become more passionate about topics in the media, situations involving friends or family, or the way people present and act in public.

Ben can become quite intimidating during his Manic state. He may swear and threatens violence against those who don't share his views.
To Ben, at the time, he does not understand that he is hurting people.

Ben often goes for long walks during his Manic state.
Sometimes he returns home hours later.
Ben claims that he calms down quicker with a change of scenery.

Ben finds that the use of medication and Therapy sessions together work best, when it comes to coping with his Bipolar Disorder.

Through therapy, Ben has learnt ways to calm his mind when he is angry.

When we are not in a Manic state, we often experience a Depressive episode. Like a Manic episode, this depressive state can last for a couple of hours or even weeks at a time.

When I feel depressed, my symptoms are so severe that they cause me to feel such sadness, guilt and loss of hope.

I begin to question; if I will ever feel normal again.

I can be seen believing in delusions or acting on impulses. Sometimes I may lash out through frustration when someone tries to control me physically.

By doing this, I feel I can show people I am hurting inside. I am also known to sleep a lot.

I do know that this is not the right course of action.
At the time I can not see this sense.

Ben experiences his depressive lows slightly differently. He has negative thoughts, as I do.

He finds it comforting to distract himself by playing video games.

Getting Ben to do anything else during his depressive episodes is like teaching a goldfish to climb a tree. Ben withdraws stubbornly.

I find it helpful when Ben talks to me about his sadness and thoughts. Often, any advice we give Ben seems to be dismissed with a negative excuse.

I persist as I love Ben and want him to know I am here for him.

Both Ben and I experience continuous feelings of guilt and anxiety. We regret the pain and frustration that We THINK we give others; when we experience our Manic or Depressive episodes.

We are told by our loved ones that we are ok and don't need to experience such feelings, but we do because we never want to hurt anyone.

we can't control when we switch moods; from Manic highs to Depressive lows. We can't be sure what triggers us to switch, how long we will be in each 'state' or what symptoms we will demonstrate.

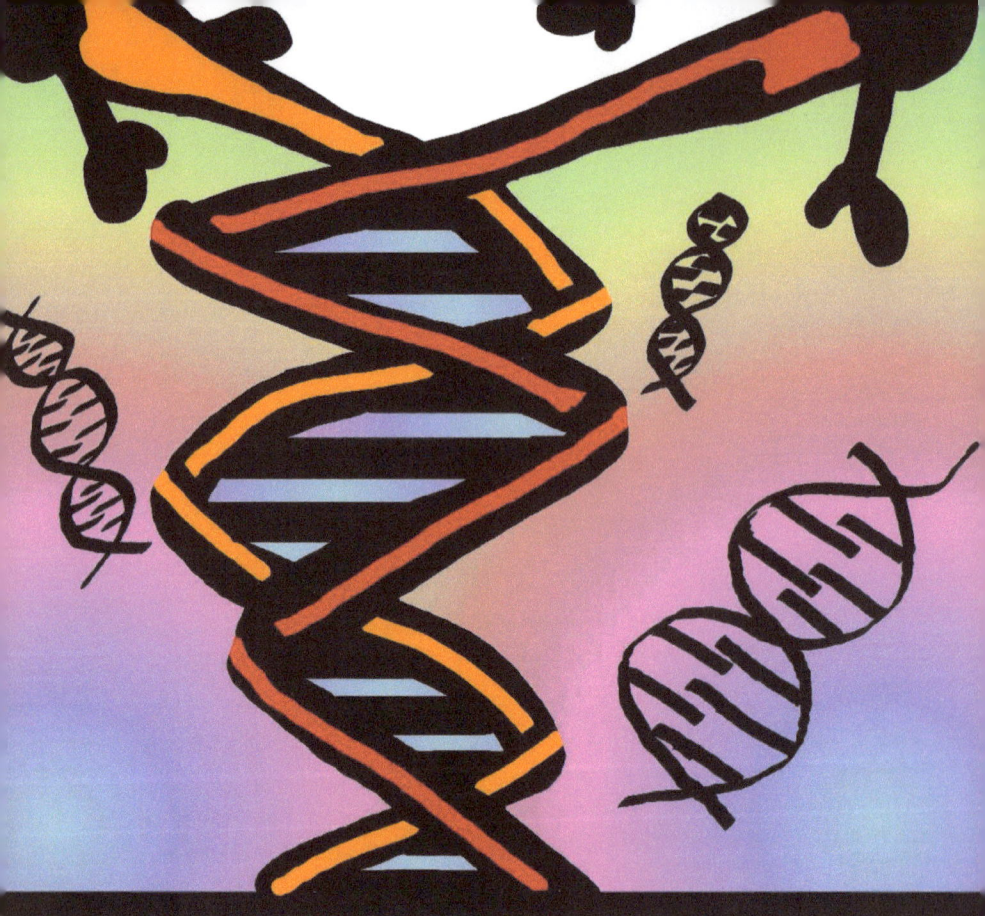

Bipolar disorder can be hereditary. Symptoms can begin to show or become more obvious at an early age, in our teens, or during our early adulthood. Early intervention can help individuals and their families cope with symptoms. Medication, Therapy, and Psychology sessions are the most effective resources to help those living with Bipolar Disorder.

We don't choose Bipolar.
We just have it.

Although a cause of Bipolar Disorder is not known, it is suspected that such symptoms are influenced by altered brain structure and chemistry, along with the environment and genetics.

If you or someone you know has Bipolar Disorder, please do not feel alone. You most certainly are not! There are many resources that you can access to help assess and manage the symptoms of Bipolar disorder. You just need to ask.

THE END

About the AUTHOR

Lady Taylor is a vision impared Australian whom identifies as an Empath and Clairscentient. After experiencing first-hand the discrimination towards Mental Illness and Disorders, within interpersonal relations, workplaces, and communal environments, Amanda identified a growing need to 'understand' the impact of such disabilities.

" The majority of information I had access to, when my symptoms developed, was based on hard-to-understand 'scientific' studies of such disorders. These seemed to structure stereotypical views of Mental Illness; supported by, I suspect, a 'taboo' stigma. I feel not much has changed regarding the general understanding of associated symptoms. I strongly feel a lack of access to reader-friendly resources allows for 'discriminatory gaps', misdiagnosis, and workplace policies/ procedures that overlook needs of the vulnerable. In turn, misunderstanding symptoms, alone, causes more acute cases of related disorders; putting lives at risk. Family-friendly resources will support early intervention strategies, structuring a healthier and stronger society."

Lady Taylor drew on the personal experiences of herself, colleagues, and relations; incoroperating them into these symptom-focused books. After circulating written and audio drafts within her community, Amanda noted the possitive impact such resources can have in a professional and interpersonal environment. Finally, Amanda teamed up with Angel Key Publications to reach a broader audience, with the goal to assist as many people as possible, to be the best version of themselves.